Artists' Workshop

Landscapes

Penny King & Clare Roundhill

 Crabtree Publishing Company

Artists' Workshop

Crabtree Publishing Company

350 Fifth Avenue	360 York Road, R.R.4	73 Lime Walk
Suite 3308	Niagara-on-the-Lake	Headington, Oxford
New York, NY 10118	Ontario L0S 1J0	England 0X3 7AD

Edited by **Bobbie Kalman**

Designed by **Jane Warring**

Illustrations by **Lindy Norton**

Children's pictures by

**Emily Ashworth, Amber Civardi, Camilla Cramsie, Louise Cramsie,
Charlotte Downham, Lara Haworth, Lucinda Howells, Sophie Johns,
Lucy MacDonald Watson, Zoë More O'Ferrall, Gussie Pownall, Thomas Stofer,
Alice Williams, Dusty Williams** Photographs by **Peter Millard**

Picture Research **by Sara Elliott**

Created by
Thumbprint Books

Copyright © 1996 Thumbprint Books

Cataloging-in-Publication Data

Roundhill, Clare, 1964-
Landscapes/Clare Roundhill & Penny King
(Artists' workshop)
Includes index.
ISBN 0-86505-853-9 (hc)   ISBN 0-86505-863-6 (pbk)
Provides inspiration for landscape painting by presenting the work of six different artists;
then offers instructions for creating one's own work.
1. Art-Technique-Juvenile literature. 2. Landscape in art-Juvenile literature.
I. King, Penny, 1963-   . II. Title. III. Series.
N8213.R59 1996   702'.8   LC 95-50840
CIP

First published in 1996 by
A & C Black (Publishers) Limited
35 Bedford Row, London WC1R 4JH

Printed and bound in Singapore

Cover Photograph:
Raoul Dufy Open Window at Saint-Jeannet (c. 1926-27)
Dufy was a French artist who painted views of regattas, racecourses, sea fronts
and other landscapes. He worked quickly, using patches of color as
a background covered with bolder strokes for detail.

Contents

Looking at landscapes

Wherever you live in the world, you will see a view when you look out of a window. You might see trees and fields, sky and clouds, a shimmering sea, or houses and shops. These views are called landscapes.

Klimt and Hundertwasser painted imaginary landscapes to show how they would like the world to be. They often used glowing colors and patterns.

In this book, there are six landscapes created by artists from different countries. Two of the artists, Monet and Hokusai, painted real places they knew well and loved. They spent a long time looking at one place at different times of the day, throughout the year, and in all kinds of weather.

O'Keeffe and Burchfield had strong feelings about the places they painted. They did not paint places exactly as they were but tried to show the special atmosphere by using unusual colors and shapes.

Landscape artists want the people who look at their pictures to feel as if they could walk into them and wander around. Sometimes they include an empty chair in their paintings so that the viewer can imagine sitting down and becoming part of the picture.

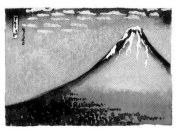

Painting a landscape is a good way of reminding yourself of a place that you have visited. Spend time looking closely at the colors, shapes and details. Decide how the place makes you feel. Does it make you feel calm or energetic, happy or sad?

One way to make a picture look like a real place is to use perspective. This means you have to paint the things closest to you bigger than those in the distance.

Notice where the land or sea appears to meet the sky. This is called the horizon.

If you prefer, paint landscapes from your imagination or from dreams, such as the picture of the upside-down houses above. Think of how an over-grown garden, alien planet or hidden city might look.

Make your picture as fantastic as you can. Exaggerate the shapes and use vivid colors.

Views of a volcano

Mount Fuji is the highest peak in Japan and one of Japan's most sacred places. People go on long and difficult journeys to visit and worship this mountain. A famous Japanese artist, called Hokusai, who lived over 200 years ago, made many wonderful woodcut prints of it.

Katsushiko Hokusai   Fuji in Clear Weather   1823-29, British Museum, London.

Hokusai created over 30,000 designs in his life, but he is probably best-known for his set of 36 prints of Mount Fuji. He made these when he was nearly 70 years old. The prints show Mount Fuji from all sides and in all kinds of weather.

Hokusai used bold colors and strong shapes in his prints. In this one, the solid red of the mountain makes it stand out against the patterns of the clouds and trees. In his famous picture, *The Wave*, Mount Fuji is painted behind a stormy sea.

1 A team of people made a woodcut print. The artist drew a sketch of the outlines on see-through paper. A block cutter pasted the sketch face down onto a block of wood. Using a knife, he cut everything away except the outline.

3 A separate block was needed for every color in the picture. Using an outline print, the artist drew in the design for each color. The block cutter cut away everything that was not this color.

2 This block was called the key block. A printer covered it with ink and put a piece of paper on top. He smoothed the paper to make sure that the whole picture was printed. He made lots of these outline prints.

4 The printer pressed a piece of paper onto each colored block in turn. Each time, he lined the paper up with the raised corner of the block, so that all the parts of the picture were in the right place.

Mighty mountains

It would take you a long time to do a woodcut like that of Hokusai. There are, however, several easy ways of making pictures that will look like woodcuts. Before you start any printing, it is a good idea to plan your picture by drawing it on a sheet of paper.

Plasticine prints

Take some Plasticine and roll it flat. Cut it into a square with a knife. Using the point of a pencil or a knitting needle, scratch a volcano in it, showing steam shooting out of the top.

Cover the volcano, steam and background with different colored poster paints. Press a piece of paper larger than your picture onto the Plasticine. Carefully peel it off. You now have a print of your picture.

Art tile prints

Scratch a picture of a mountain in the middle of an art tile. Cover the slopes with trees and some houses. Put stars and a moon in the sky. Coat the tile with printing ink and press a piece of paper onto it. Peel the paper off. Let the ink dry before recoating the tile with another color.

Mount Fuji erupts

Imagine you are in Japan about 300 years ago, when Mount Fuji last erupted. Paint a picture of how you imagine the mountain must have looked. Use reds, oranges and yellows for the flames and dark gray for the lava and smoke.

Golden garden

This glowing, golden tree with its twisting, curling branches is a sketch for part of a huge mural designed by Gustav Klimt, a famous Austrian artist. The finished picture was created in a long mosaic of marble inlaid with gold, enamel and semi-precious stones.

Gustav Klimt The Tree of Life c.1905–1909. Österreichisches Museum für Angewandte Kunst, Vienna

Klimt wanted the frieze to seem magical and fantastic. He made a careful and detailed sketch for the mosaic maker to follow. Klimt used paints, crayons and colored shapes as well as real gold and silver leaf in his design.

The mosaic was made to decorate the dining room of Adolphe Stoclet, a very rich man who lived in Brussels. The two huge panels, which face one another, each have a tree as the main image. One is the Tree of Knowledge and the other is the Tree of Life.

Under one of the two big trees is a dancing girl and under the other is a man and a woman hugging. Klimt wanted to show a magical world where people could always be happy.

These people have normal-looking heads and hands, but their clothes are covered with jewel-like patterns. Klimt was more interested in decoration than in trying to make people and objects look real and three-dimensional.

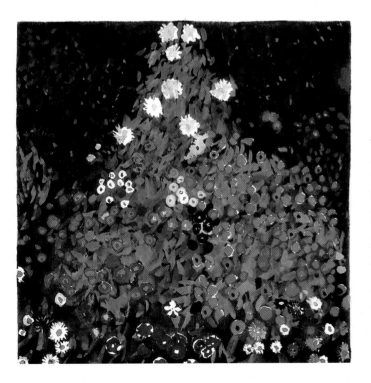

When he was older, Klimt did not like to talk much and preferred to spend his time alone. One of the most important things in his life was his garden, which gave him many ideas for paintings. This is a picture of his garden in bloom. The flowers fill every bit of the space on his canvas.

Trees and flowers

Design your own magical Tree of Life with golden branches covered in delicious fruit or paint a picture of a happy person dancing in a fantastic garden. You could also create a garden full of wild and wonderful flowers reaching up to the sun.

The Tree of Life

Draw a tree with curling, twisting branches on a big piece of gold paper. Cut it out and glue it onto a bright-colored background. Make a mosaic path with small squares and triangles cut from different colored shiny paper.

Cut out curved tin-foil leaves, juicy felt fruits and colorful wiggly paper shapes to decorate your tree. You might like to add some pretty birds perching in the branches.

A merry dancer

In the middle of a sheet of paper, draw a happy picture of a dancer, wearing loose clothes and leaping with delight.

Make the head, hands and feet look as realistic as possible but decorate the clothes with fantastic patterns to give them a fairy-tale look. Like Klimt, you can use anything you want—crayons, paint, shiny mosaic pieces, or gold and silver paper.

Draw, paint, or use paper cutouts to decorate the background with flowers, bushes and long grass.

Mosaic flower bed

Practice drawing flowers on scrap paper. Make some big, fat petals, long pointed petals, and tiny petals.

Then draw flowers like these on brightly colored paper. Cut them out and stick them onto a colored background.

Add leaves and wiggly stems. Fill the whole page with flowers, leaves and tangled stems.

The waterlily pond

This picture was painted by Claude Monet, a French artist. When he was an old man, Monet spent a lot of time painting pictures of the lily pond with its Japanese bridge in his garden at Giverny, France. This is just one of 18 views of the bridge that he painted in 1899.

Claude Monet The Waterlily Pond 1899, The National Gallery, London

Monet was one of a group of artists called the Impressionists. They painted everyday scenes, often out of doors. Impressionists did not paint what they saw in detail. They were more interested in catching the effects of light on a scene.

Monet painted this same view of the lily pond at different times—in sunny and cloudy weather and in the morning and evening. He wanted to show how the look and mood of a place changed in different light.

Monet painted quickly. When art critics first saw his pictures, they thought they looked unfinished.

He used dots and dashes of color to give the impression of flowers, leaves and rippling water. He painted longer, wider strokes for bigger areas such as buildings.

Monet never used black. For shadows, he either mixed dark colors or used complementary ones.

Look at this color wheel. Red, blue and yellow, the pure colors, are called primary colors. The complementary colors are orange, green and purple. Each one is a mixture of the two primary colors on either side. Try mixing them yourself.

Woods and water

Paint some pictures of outdoor places that you know and enjoy, such as a garden, woods or lake. You don't need to put in every detail of exactly how they look. Instead, create a colorful scene that shows other people what these places might feel like.

Shimmering water

When Monet painted water, he used streaks of color to show ripples. He used white and different shades of yellow to show the glint and sparkle of sunshine on the water's surface. He used dark greens and blues for the reflections of trees and bushes. With poster paints and a fat paintbrush, use Monet's techniques to create your own picture of shimmering water. Add pretty water lilies or some shadowy reflections of trees.

Autumn colors

Paint a glowing autumn picture of a tree or a whole forest, with leaves in shades of orange, yellow, red and brown. Don't bother to paint every leaf. Do as the Impressionists did. Paint a knobby tree trunk with branches and then dab on overlapping splotches of autumn colors for the leaves.

A flowery garden

Mix as many different shades of green as you can. Use them to paint a picture of a leafy garden. Blend the colors into one another, brushing in different directions to make your picture look alive. Use dark colors for shadows and light colors for the brighter places. Dot bright pink, red, blue, orange and yellow flowers all over your garden.

Spectacular sunrise

Have you ever been awake early enough to see the sun rising? This picture by an American artist called Georgia O'Keeffe is her idea of a spectacular sunrise in Texas. She loved to be out early in the wide open spaces with the sky towering above her.

Georgia O'Keeffe Sunrise with Little Clouds No II 1916, Private Collection

O'Keeffe has used only the primary colors (red, blue and yellow), which she has mixed together to create the glowing colors of the sky. There are three parts to the picture—the top shows the night sky and the bottom, the dark ground. The rising sun in the middle of the painting brightens up the whole scene.

In her painting, O'Keeffe has shown the sky and clouds, but she has used unusual colors and shapes, taken from her imagination. Although some people might think that this picture just looks like a sandwich of color, others can easily spot the sun rising at the beginning of a new day.

Georgia O'Keeffe grew up in the countryside, but later she went to live in New York. She lived in an apartment on the 28th floor of the very first skyscraper that was built there. She was so excited about the tall buildings of New York that she painted over 20 pictures of them, often showing them at night. This famous O'Keeffe painting is called the American Radiator Building.

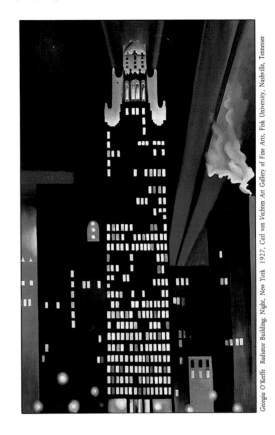

Georgia O'Keeffe Radiator Building: Night, New York 1927, Carl von Vechten Art Gallery of Fine Arts, Fisk University, Nashville, Tennessee

The artist is best known for her pictures of flowers. She painted them very close up so that every detail and shade of color could be seen. It seems almost as if she was looking through a magnifying glass as she painted.

Every year, O'Keeffe went to her house in New Mexico. While she was there, she started to paint pictures of the bones of animals that had died in the desert. She particularly liked the contrasting look of the stark white bones against the bright blue sky. Her husband and friends often found themselves sharing the car with piles of bones that she had collected.

Sensational skies

Georgia O'Keeffe did not believe in simply copying the landscapes that she saw. She liked to use her imagination and feelings to help make her paintings unusual and exciting. Paint your own sunset pictures and make them as dreamlike as O'Keeffe made her pictures.

Rolling clouds

Look up at the sky when the sun is just setting. Use pastels or chalk to sketch the clouds that you can see. Start by making the clouds white. To make gray clouds, add a little black. Add red to show the sunset.

Blend the colors with your finger or a small cotton ball. Don't worry if the clouds look a bit unreal—the more magical they look, the better.

Spectacular sunrise

You need to use only the three primary colors—red, blue and yellow—to make this spectacular sunrise. Using a fat brush, wet a piece of paper all over with water. Imagine that your piece of paper is divided into three parts.

Over the top third of your paper, paint purple-blues for the sky and reds for the clouds. In the middle, use lighter oranges and yellows to show that the day is just beginning. On the bottom, paint a rich earth, rippling sea or rolling hills.

Remember that you are painting an imaginary picture. Work quickly and don't worry about making it look exactly like real life.

Far horizons

The horizon is the place where the sky seems to touch the land. To create your own horizon painting, first fold a piece of paper in half.

Over the top half, paint a dark sky with big black clouds and bolts of lightning zig-zagging down to the ground. Paint fields over the bottom half.

When your painting is dry, add some trees. Make them small or large and put them in the horizon or foreground.

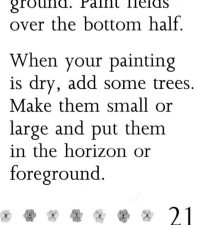

A frosty forest

This forest, shown on a freezing-cold night, was painted with watercolors by an American artist called Charles Burchfield. Although he has used only a few colors, the artist has managed to catch the wintry feeling.

Charles E. Burchfield *Orion in December* 1959, National Museum of American Art, Washington D.C.

Earth and sky seem to meet in Burchfield's picture. You can see that some of the stars have been painted among the trees. The trees are outlined in black, which gives them a slightly ghostly feeling.

The stars in the sky look like the twinkling snowflakes on the frosty ground. Burchfield has made them shimmer and sparkle by giving each of them a contrasting black outline and a halo of white paint.

When Burchfield was a young boy, he liked to go for long walks in the forest. He noticed the patterns and light all around him. Sometimes, to help him to concentrate, he lay on the ground with his eyes shut tight.

Burchfield enjoyed the sound of the wind whistling through the trees, the smell of the forest and the feel of the ground beneath him. When he became an artist, he used the powerful memories of his visits to the woods to paint many of his pictures.

In his painting, Burchfield has shown a constellation of stars called Orion. In Greek mythology, Orion was a hunter. He was accidentally killed by a goddess, called Artemis. Artemis was so sorry about what she had done that she turned Orion into a constellation of stars so that he would always be remembered.

If you look carefully, you can see that the three stars in a row show Orion's belt, and two big stars are his huge shoulders.

23

Winter wonders

Imagine that it's late at night and everything is still and silent. Delicate snowflakes are falling on the dark, leafless trees, and the stars are glimmering in the sky. Paint a picture of how you think this would look, using the same wintry colors as Burchfield.

Moonlit scene

Use white, black, blue and brown to paint a landscape scene in the middle of a dark night. Add a starry sky and a shining moon. Make the stars shimmer by giving them contrasting outlines. Think about the pale night-time colors and the silence all around. Give your picture a mysterious feeling.

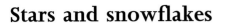

Stars and snowflakes

To create these incredible snowflakes and stunning stars, you'll need a water-based black felt-tipped pen and some absorbent paper towel or blotting paper.

Cut the paper into circles or squares. Draw star or snowflake shapes on the paper with the felt-tipped pen and then drip water onto your picture. As the water spreads over the surface, it will make the black ink split into a rainbow of colors.

Scratchboard snow scene

For this technique, you'll need a scratchboard and scraper tool, which can be bought in an art shop.

Make a sketch of the scene you are going to create. Draw the outline of a forest full of bare trees. Add flurries of snowflakes and some twinkling stars. Complete your picture with stiff, frosty grass.

Use the scraping tool to scratch your winter landscape on the scratchboard. Don't worry if you make a mistake, as it is very easy to turn the mark into something else.

Happy houses

How would you like to live in one of these brilliantly colored, crazy-looking houses? The artist who created them is an Austrian called Friedrich Hundertwasser. He feels that if people live in bright and cheerful homes, they have happier and more interesting lives.

Hundertwasser 637a Waiting Houses 1969

To Hundertwasser, color is the most important thing. He feels that heaven must be a colorful, bright place, whereas hell must be dull and gray. He always frames his pictures in black because he thinks it makes the colors shine like jewels.

The artist often signs his pictures with different names. He has signed this picture of a row of domed houses, 'Regentag', which means 'rainy day'. He chose this name because he loves to look at bright colors sparkling through the rain.

Hundertwasser has designed and built many houses. This is a famous one he built in Vienna, called 'Hundertwasserhaus'.

He wanted to build homes for ordinary people that were as fantastic and dreamlike as the palaces built for kings. Each apartment is completely different, and none of the doors and windows is the same. Hundertwasser planted trees on top of the building to give shade and color as well as to clean the air.

This unusual artist often adds colorful onion-shaped domes to the houses he designs or paints.

They look just like the domes on this beautiful building in Moscow, called Saint Basil's Cathedral. He thinks the onion shape means wealth and happiness.

Dreamlike dwellings

Imagine that you have been asked to design some houses. You can use really bright colors and put the doors and windows wherever you like. The roofs can have plants growing on them or they can be shaped like vegetables or fruit.

Swirly houses

Use some bright jewel-like colors to paint a row of houses. Mix the three primary colors—red, yellow and blue—as well as black and white. Look at the color wheel on page 15 for tips on mixing.

Add some glue and flour to the paint to make it thick and shiny. Cut out a small rectangle of stiff cardboard. Snip zigzags in one end. This will make a paint comb.

Paint one house at a time on separate pieces of paper. Before the paint dries, scrape swirly patterns in it with your paint comb. Cut out the houses and glue them on black bristol board. Add shiny windows.

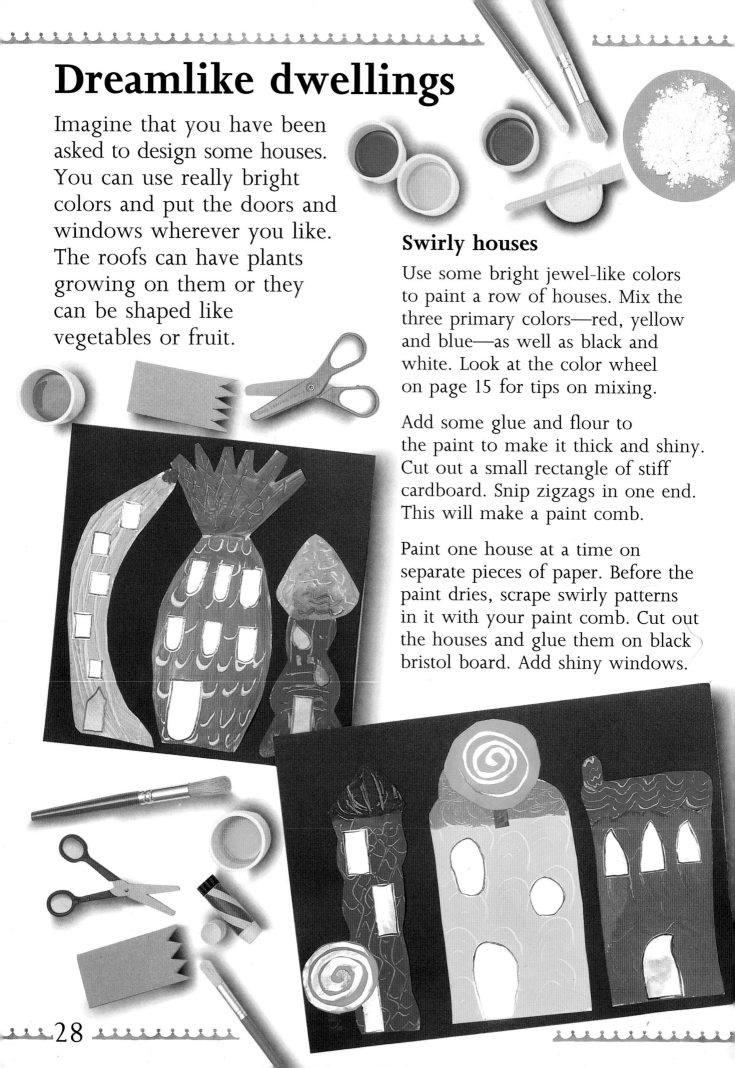

Twinkly palace

Collect fake fur, sequins, scraps of brightly colored fabric and felt to make this palace. Colored pipe cleaners are perfect for the swirls. Use a piece of shiny paper for the background.

Decorate your palace with fur fabric. Add odd-shaped towers cut out of fabric or paper. Decorate them with sequins, pipe-cleaners and glitter. Glue a sun or moon and some stars all over the background.

Soaring skyscraper

Hundertwasser often paints buildings with lots of windows in different shapes and sizes. Look at the windows in your town. How many shapes did you see?

Using a dark felt-tipped pen, draw the outline of a skyscraper. Cut out and glue on silver foil windows. Outline the windows with another dark color. Use brightly-colored felt-tipped pens to decorate your building.

29

More about the artists

Katsushika Hokusai
(1760 - 1849   Japanese)
Fuji in Clear Weather 1823-29)

Hokusai became an artist's assistant at the age of 15 and worked as an artist for more than 70 years. Some of his best work was done when he was a very old man, over 80. He is best-known for his landscapes, but he also illustrated books, designed greetings cards and drew many portraits. He enjoyed painting huge mythological figures being watched by crowds of spectators at festivals.

Gustav Klimt
(1826 - 1918   Austrian)
The Tree of Life c.1905-1909

Gustav Klimt came from a family of artists. He and his brother ran a business painting pictures on the interiors of people's houses and great buildings, such as in theaters, museums and the University of Vienna. He later became famous for painting portraits of rich society women. Klimt also designed fabrics, dresses and jewelry.

Claude Monet
(1840 - 1926   French)
The Waterlily Pond 1899

Monet often painted out of doors, showing views of the countryside, the seaside or boats on the river. He also painted pictures of railway stations, cathedrals and buildings in cities. He often did a series of pictures of the same view, such as haystacks or poplar trees. He wanted to show how these views changed in different light. During the last forty years of his life, he created a magnificent garden at Giverny, in France, and painted many pictures of its exotic flowers.

Georgia O'Keeffe
(1887 - 1986   American)
Sunrise with Little Clouds No II 1916)

Georgia O'Keeffe decided that she wanted to become an artist when she was still a child. The scenery and objects that she saw on her many travels inspired most of her pictures. O'Keeffe liked to paint outside, and she is best known for her detailed pictures of flowers, shells, rocks and pieces of wood. She also painted incredible bird's-eye views of rivers, roads and rolling clouds. She remembered the way they looked when she saw them out of airplane windows.

Charles Burchfield
(1893 - 1967   American)
Orion in December 1959

Burchfield's early paintings are scenes of Ohio, the place where he grew up. He believed that looking hard at landscapes would help him understand God. He liked to concentrate on the sounds, smells and sights of nature and tried to show its power in his paintings. For a time, he worked as a designer in a wallpaper factory, which made him particularly interested in patterns.

Friedrich Hundertwasser
(Born 1928   Austrian)
Waiting Houses 1969

Hundertwasser's work is inspired by nature. He hopes that his pictures might help make the world a more peaceful place. He puts trees and grass on top of the buildings he creates and never uses straight lines in his paintings because they don't exist in nature. He recycles materials, often painting on used envelopes and making his own clothes and shoes from scraps of fabric.

Other things to do

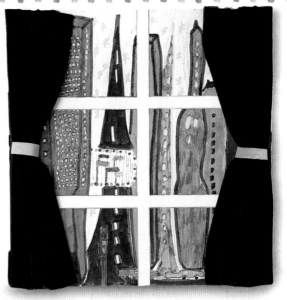

1 Make a textured landscape print. Sketch a picture on a large sheet of paper. Find objects with textures, such as leaves, a sponge, string, cotton ball and corrugated paper. Press them one at a time into poster paint and then onto scrap paper. See what patterns they make. Print the patterns you like best onto your landscape picture.

3 On some cardboard, draw or paint your favorite view. Make a window frame for it by gluing long strips of paper onto it. Add curtains made of fabric or tissue paper. Hang the picture on your bedroom wall to look like an extra window.

2 Build a fantastic model landscape of an alien planet. Is your planet hot or cold, dry or wet? Do the plants have big leaves or none at all? What colors are they? Imagine the shape, size and materials of the buildings. Use scrunched-up paper, foil, and other odds and ends.

4 Paint a mural for your bedroom wall on a roll of shelf paper or on the back of some spare wallpaper. Imagine you are standing on top of a mountain and that you can see views all around you. There may be hills, rivers, forests, mountains, towns or big cities.

Index

Acknowledgements
The publishers are grateful to the following institutes and individuals for permission to reproduce the illustrations on the pages mentioned.
Tate Gallery, London/© DACS: cover; British Museum, London: 6; Österreichisches Museum für Angewandte Kunst, Vienna: 10; Reproduced by courtesy of the Trustees, The National Gallery, London: 14; Photo by Malcolm Varon, NYC/The Georgia O'Keeffe Foundation, Abiquiu, New Mexico/© DACS: 18; Carl Van Vechten Art Gallery, Fisk University, Nashville: 19; National Museum of American Art, Washington DC/Art Resource, NY: 22; © 1996 Joram Harel, Vienna, Austria: 26.